Scofflaw

OTHER BOOKS BY GARRY THOMAS MORSE

POETRY

After Jack
Discovery Passages
Prairie Harbour
Safety Sand
Streams
Transversals for Orpheus

FICTION

Death in Vancouver

THE CHAOS! QUINCUNX SERIES

Minor Episodes / Major Ruckus
Rogue Cells / Carbon Harbour
Minor Expectations
Yams Do Not Exist

ScOFF-LAW

GARRY THOMAS MORSE

POEMS

anvil press • vancouver

Library and Archives Canada Cataloguing in Publication

Title: Scoff-law : poems / Garry Thomas Morse.
Other titles: Scofflaw
Names: Morse, Garry Thomas, author.
Identifiers: Canadiana 20210130857 | ISBN 9781772141726 (softcover)
Subjects: LCSH: Indigenous peoples—Poetry.
Classification: LCC PS8626.O774 S36 2021 | DDC C811/.6—dc23

Cover design by Rayola.com
Cover painting by KC Adams
Interior layout by HeimatHouse

Represented in Canada by Publishers Group Canada
Distributed in Canada by Raincoast Books
Distributed in the USA by Small Press Distribution (SPD)

The publisher gratefully acknowledges the financial assistance of the Canada Council
for the Arts, the Canada Book Fund, and the Province of British Columbia through
the B.C. Arts Council and the Book Publishing Tax Credit.

Anvil Press Publishers Inc.
P.O. Box 3008, Main Post Office
Vancouver, B.C. V6B 3X5 Canada
www.anvilpress.com

PRINTED AND BOUND IN CANADA

TABLE OF CONTENTS

Name Yr Poison / 7

No-Brainer / 11

Extinct Pennies / 15

Chemistry Metrics / 19

Smudge / 21

Dream Snatcher / 24

Autofocus / 28

Cliffhanger / 29

Hate Waste / 38

Calling All Scofflaws / 45

Global Transplant / 46

Puncture / 49

Bot Russe / 53

The Other Side (I) Seen / 58

Acknowledgments / 71

NAME YR POISON

We'd heard it all before but sit yourself down with a
facial tissue or two.
                    Bound to be
pseudotragic, this primitive diatribe felt for stress
                            & strain in every section. No way
to cram our specialized *tsuris* into carved

                            niche or crude
                                        aftermath of historical
hiccups.
        Pffft...speaking of which, the new pesticides are too
pricey this summer. What kind of town where them sumbitches
can drink in public from
                        a dandelion? The other afternoon plain as a
nose on a face, that tawny-edged skipper clung
                        to a purple shoot like Nobody's
Business. We tell our amigo
            quit trying to make vetch happen. Won't sleep a wink
till that disturbed area is history. Tear up
                        by the roots anything
that stirs, bathe in blue light, bask in scenes of a greenish square
prepare the spare
                tabula rasa
                    clean enough to eat off of

What time the show begin?

Acquainted at best with that teller of tall tales, we sink
a few in endangered joints with bedroom views in the
works. Can still hear the Weakerthans from the
backroom
        can still hear
ourselves not think. Maybe tear
                down those idle stretches of

repurposed blot-outs. Name of progress.

        Game to
             try our hand at commodities
    like organic *affect*
        & free range amnesia.

                    STRUM

Listen, before you can say "ululation" he's on you, plying
his trade something terrible

        quick hands brown

    from the sun

     or circumstance of a difficult birth.

            (Don't ask.)

Calls himself Scofflaw

        with a voice that cracks into that

      insectile

        rasp through rushes, you hear

          through centuries of sheer innovation.

After the first mow see sweet clover fly up about his bare feet...

        Stands to reason there's a picture window
alongside Jean Brébeuf where Scofflaw steps into the
      frame.
      Black
        swallowtails flit by.

Early one morning

        he shows us a long row of chrysalises, each
from a silken

      hook suspending

      disbelief.

Each shell's the same shade as the

        substrate, or so he says, keep them
peepers peeled for translucence, a hint of wet wings before
eclosion.

Whatever. Exterminate the brutes, or at least that wretched
European Skipper, a colonial threat to our trade in

                                             timothy

    seed   feed of champions

                              prizegetters, outside

                                        longshots.

      Meanwhile, our neighbour humblebrags
      about the best poison for the dandelion
      menace.

We expect it might come to blows, but Scofflaw's eyes
    brim
        over. In his worldview, grasshoppers are

            kosher, easily gulled, delicious

            between marked-up, unleavened

            what have you

not to mention

    the way Athenian women wore fake cicadas

    to show they had sprung from the soil

    rocks & trees

    flaunting the virtue of being

                  autochthones.

Well, that shuts us the fuck up.

NO-BRAINER

We've been round these parts for as long as any
body can remember. The land was grandparented
   down

       & before then   our seed
   blew

      about   like fluff off a female
poplar. Pussy

    willow, sniffs Scofflaw, a first

    world problem for certain.

He's got none too high an opinion of our whole

freaking deal.

       Nothing's to be made

          out of turf that won't

                 till.

Digression becomes him
even that quip about Beethoven
               answering the "landowner"
     under his name
           signing "brain-holder"
or Scofflaw's contrary claim: pre
    occupation

with the savage mind   subject

to geographical amscray.   By now

    we know climate change, not that climate

    changes us, affects

        our neuroplasticity   in other words
                 brains us

                something wicked.

Scofflaw might as well be hectoring in the
                Attic, talking Empedocles, or
teasing us with echoes of Aeolic murmurations for all his efforts to
impress upon us
      furtive rearrangements of the furniture

      in his headspace carried by charges of im-
minent storm or masses of warm

              air that imbue our
slightest mishaps with emotional intensity.

                Negative
        ions, not negative capability, to sew up
    his {SILLA jism} or what have you.

             See among the
    tortoiseshells sipping
          willow the nightmare of
any copy-editor worth
        her salt

a stray   comma

on the wrong side of the

tracks.

Scofflaw says that some
of those glitter-winged
                    critters   puddle

              in clusters   to build up

              salt for   sperm

ie. a male monarch has no body
                              politic

      when he's fixing to duplicate

      bearing north in three

                              generations. Before latex
there was *Asclepias*, cribbed for our pleasure
      milkweed, the food
          they follow, the stuff they need to toxify

          themselves.

Migration's hardly our priority—given
                              the tug of umbilicals
      our kids clambering out of caked
earth with a sense of dominion over all wingèd
                        things
          fancy toast down

                  their fronts.

Quit lollygagging, Scofflaw.

You'll put the little ones off their feed. What about the stone

that clove to let you the northern lights

                                that hunk

of labradorite

                spruces up your desk
                with primal immanence. Think of a
                stone hammer passed from hand
                                        to hand

then try not to

what in the trade we call a
                        no-brainer.

                                Copy that?

EXTINCT PENNIES

You can't teach an old dog not to toss out recycling
(knotted in plastic) nor a bear not to exfoliate
with a hella big rock
nor the likes of us

the way a little bit of Schnittke

can up the ante.

Our recidivist chum clears

throat, kicks lectern aside

rails against corn-fed media

for calling prairie grasses

uncultivated

       "farmland"

Listen, in that string quartet, the sense of dread
strikes us as cringey
                our sweetheart deal to extradite
dissident organs
            via whims of the free market
twenty shades of
          totalitarianism
              another *agitato*
life hack cracking up over relentless
             metronome.

So goes the polystylism of the Self

Pardoner's tale, another stir-fried apology presaging the
movement about to seize the nation by its short

term memory—

                    Whoa…the auto-acknowledgment
                    dictates a moment of prayer for the pipeline
extension that funded this mundane
                                        dog & pony
maybe a slow clap for clean-up crew

taxed into making this finger food

spread reality

                    not merely theory. Scofflaw

            shears grass ceiling

            ignites some sage to bless

the territory

        for saying "no" but meaning "yes"
by no means the first to drink the

            Fool-Aid (for only pennies a glass).

Before his vitals are auctioned off
he could tutor a wax moth
caterpillar to snack back on plastic
or an intestinal nematode to eat up
crude spillage

shinny up the traumatic bottleneck
                                swilling illustrateds
from the '70s Rebellion, shooting past looting Natives
depicted as lounging
                        beneath tricoloured sun
                        umbrellas.

Even the tentative footbridge of e-reconciliation is built
upon the bones of crushed workers
buried in the comments:

                        weird how a synthetic

                        thread in 10,000,000

                        environmental tees

                        will end the planet

        In summary, sorry (not sorry) for what was said
during the public apology…

Anything with more meat

than a sound bite would

soundly slap him out

                        of this hysterical fiction—with Idyll
No More showing record numbers
storming the one-track Train of Thought

                                from sea to sea.

They're doing Ubu this year
sampling Ube to cool off
(sweet tuber treats)

according to our town crier

plagued by flies

for his kinship with nature

for his station in the New World.

      In the scheme of things, we never knew no man to have
such a non-smell. Dogs would stop to lick the fur along the backs of
his legs. Shame we ever pegged him as a projection of our schisma-
tism— sorry—our stigmatism, no longer able to hear that trill in post-
humous nocturne over the crunch of
                          remains giving us
                                  grief.

On the usual hike home, a tourist stops us to ask if the swath of
green is an Indian graveyard, meaning to leave it intact like that.

      Scofflaw bares crowded teeth

& spits

      reckons it has endured a

                railroad.

CHEMISTRY METRICS

A clatter of yellow light rouses us after Daylight Savings.

With *Träumerei*
between our ears
lemon-scented, held over

open mouth, likely the

chloroform in liquid
        fabric   softener or dryer sheets, riffing on

conceptual list poem:
        benzyl acetate benzyl alcohol ethanol yummy limonene

or the aforementioned carcinogen/neurotoxin
flouting scent-free policy, nilling us softly.

        Pardon our parrhesia about the view from
below the poverty line—singing in the shower
                  nearly took a
                      tumble
    hearing the right
    to drinking water
    going

        down the drain

        swabbing

        Scofflaw's fingerwag

for the dash of

Indian
                    hemoglobin he periodically laid claim to
the word queued for deletion in 30 days.

In the background a celebratory
                              drone
about the death of natural grasslands
canola grown, the proceeds gone
towards canned goods
thanks to grass/roots
                    extirpation

Th' imposthume of much wealth
                        by harvest time, our yield will be
on the table, exchanged for the innards of ignorables.

Accept there are things
the language of prairie dogs cannot explain.

SMUDGE

Somewhere in this brain [not my department]

that sudden surge of

                dopamine makes
a dope out of you
           & me amid Beaux-Arts

       limestone, moving through

       Union Station

           laughing at fossils, suffering that odd
affliction AKA
      HAPPINESS
             fingering trigger to glutamate
backlash, itchy to break from collective
    discantus
cry the shock of wet socks in field of staticky feedback:

             "Imagine a
        commodity fetish wrapped in a Bay blanket

coat" why Mind falters when aiming to

       outdraw these eleMenTal conditions, why Mouth
redresses proud tradition of striped bikini upon ethically sourced
           coyote fur scatter rug
   REVERSIBLE
for any spillage, or historically, mess
for descendants to tidy up

scat · o · log · i · cal

catfish

tossed back into the Seine

our small tributary our *voyageur solitaire* forever
Othered among sleepwalkers for whom

Nutty Club
Man cares

the more   COSCO CHINA

IMPORTS

shunt into territory looking inward

to lake fish farm dream, petting sturgeon
with lapels shaken
       in rage: "You knew the bones

            were there when you

               built the museum!"

with verismo pantomime
scratched into repo-land
queries with decorum
         whether the edifice is

       haunted by

           brute injustice or

    artiFACTS

of our existence   haunted by that friendly

        penetration of

          sky.

On apologetic holidays, our eidetic self
                    wraps selfsame self
in eiderdown & glosses Indigenous loss

SMUDGED

            right out of Heidegger-y

Dasein. Scofflaw surfaces at the Ethnohistory
                                        "do"
with tobacco in his
                            pouch   female sage in his
                            hair with that auratic
quality unique to stolen
                pictures.   The bilingual *deus ex*

                    machina

                        preps us for
                    spiral
            ascent   **ASSENT**   .

    before we
    plunge

    through

    atrocity

    exhibit

        find ourselves out in the cold (again)

snow falling on shoulders of a charitably scarfed Gandhi
his sculpted state of appall unless that is a subzero shrug

            celebrated for perpetuity.

DREAM SNATCHER

after/before john newlove

fall off any horizon stuff that in your vape & toke it

not another word about fields of pure yellow

watching pain dry chewing yellowcake

impromptu sundance choreographed to jump

scare warning, another ricochet between stereotypes

pitching woo at the belle of the chitkicker's ball

fall off any horizon with the wampum of squandered memory

reread the scrip [insert stage direction

for straight-shooters rightin' wrongs]

drum up fashion-conscious headdress

indians carefully petrified in that country

the perfect regift for dustbowl rustication

the perfect product for turtle island

crafted locally or thereabouts

from kelp skirt to elk stew

now turn the other cheekbone

virtue meme the peeps who made your clothes & phone

painstakingly ground into chalk

fall off any horizon the geronimo's a real nosedive

off the edge

           of   square   prairie

brown-nose connoisseur niche

swallow the latest stats

service with a smile for the signatories of history

truth the quantum curvature of retinal distress

fall off any horizon where no one can hear you breech-cloth

wild nights, wild nights, out creep the creeps

indians, settlers, cabbies, cops, mad for contact

characters who love you (roughly)

fall off any horizon see if the body will be curated

reconciled by all accounts—

step right up, see the grandiloquent pretendian ply his truck

look for the symbol of authenticity under the foundation

reconstruct those amazing technicolour bloodlines

till a hatchet-job of interest crops up

say the names, say the claims, say the cultural frames

make the cuts then dramatize that perfect demise

trustfall into blanched snowbank of a clean, well-lighted legend

fall off any horizon no one will notice

your agency caught in the crossfire

no pressure to compact the cronyism with a firm hand-snake

unctuous to the touch—this double-headed slither

drowned in its undrinkability, drowned out

these dreams of manifest destiny in baleful chinook

snatched away by raiding parties in hazy clobber

fall for any horizon while supplies last

AUTOFOCUS

Picture in the preterite or pluperfect our petulant ambassador
truculent about
                    his initiative for a Nation
wide cooperative—cannibalization of corporate bodies
potluck diet of diversity divestment group
nibbles of sympathetic ears
pressed against Claude glass, manufacturing picturesque
lakeside
            cloning Indigeneity for generations
on night class whiteboard

                    the *con/efficiens* in **COEFFICIENT**

the Latin for signaways in triplicate.

            The second Scofflaw's elegies for bedroom burb

collapse, we see

                    a guy gulling gulls with his toy plane. A red

                        tailed hawk takes refuge in a tree nearby
reflects on history's
                    remote idiocy, absentee landlordism
whisper after whisper

                    tumbleweeding by...

        cadenzas for the mother tongue
                                    in trouble.

CLIFFHANGER

If (I)'s got character in the third person
like a task force nodding off at the switch
at the vibrating twitch
                            put (I) back in the saddle
of the highest stud in tar/Nation
with a steady CLOMP
        CLOMP.

                        Doctor Goggles 'oogles the issue on his
creaky digital assistant. He & (I)
                            had never quite seen eye to eye.
Nothing personal, he was just up to his eyes in genotypes
                            & leased luxury hybrids, probing equations

down to the roots of our unintelligible design, the toll of our
Pavlovian reactions, the troll of our erotic robotics, the goal

of our neurotic narcotics, the lossy knoll of our neurotoxicity.

                        High time to sprinkle drink

on the angel-face of Poster Boy (AKA Good Kid) & give
him a good shake.
                A presentable lad, well-spoken if a shade
green for this are-you-with-us-or-not kind of world.

This ain't
Banff, the good doctor cries.
                    You'd best ride out before sunrise caresses
the ryegrasses. Make a detour yonder by way of Drumheller & drum up
what bones you require.
                    Now in Li Po fashion, our hypothetical

horses neigh *buh-bye.*

                    A tear strikes dirt & Good Kid
                        trundles off, hanging on to his novelty
                        boleadora all through the cinematic
        ellipses…

                    Oats & water, hollers Good Kid on the other
side, brushing dust from his vest. He pulls up a stool
                                        & eyebrows
        Scofflaw over his under-cooked plate of *duelos y quebrantos*
scoping around for the nearest Dulcinea.

                    Quit these clam-fisted quixotics, Scofflaw. The

Coalition is a-coming. Just watch your family totems don't get
railroaded. Best look lively before (I) gets the drop on you.

        Form a posse of scofflaws

        or knock back a heap of

        hemlock. Just sayin'.

Out of the blue Fifth Horseman makes
raspberry noises, adding to that bad case of the giggles egged on by the
how-to on every passing boxcar:

DO NOT HAMMER   **USE VIBRATORS**

Shush, you'll wake up Totes In-Appropes.
Sadly, a bubble in the
suburbs had deprived him of more traditional acquaintanceship.
With bow & feathers, there was nothing to play but Oligarchs
& Plutocrats. No one had learned him to spear
fish on Indian Days aglow in the Rockies of a framed CPR print
as a fer instance.

Totes rubs the holes in the snow that pass for his eyes
but no ideas

spring into the fray. Too early to make our half-baked
"Duels & Ruptures" or scrappy rashers repeat

on us. Besides, Good Kid's stuffed to the gills
& chomping at the bit to get this

show on the road.

Leave behind the windmills of your
mind, Scofflaw.

(I)'s got a list as long as your arm

with enough sociological bafflegab to knock you

                                        into next week.
Scofflaw snorted between chews.

                    I will not exchange one knife for another.

        Totes In-Appropes looks up that quote from the least
adulterated of the Icelandic Sagas
                            & covers his mouth, lest
        food be taken out of it.
                            I'd rather be a ragged clause in
the small print of a totalitarian decree. Easy, chief. Try not to
get bogged down with land, lineage, or legacy.

                                    Why not reconcile

the whole hashpling today?

                        (I) can even get Tonto Toronto on the

blower. Let the market take care of itself.

                                    Lady Lifehacker looks up

from nuts she's shelling

                        upon the sawdust to give the joint

an autonomous sensory

                meridian response ambience.

Scofflaw, pry

the wax out of them

patronizing, patriarchal ears. Eleven Dictates are posted

in plain sight. Writing by committee is now

the law of the land.

FYI: (I) is

galloping down the

gutter while our gums are a-flappin'.

This just in: history's been won in a monumental

crap game.

Visible in the cross-hairs of cross-pollina-
tion keeping him awake, Scofflaw plants his feet in the
sawdust

& says even if he's a goner, he's quits with the
Union.

Yeah, but they ain't done with you, Friend-O.

Nickel's worth of advice. Big Other is one prickly
mother to tangle with. You stand to see that smug
pancake wiped right off your mug, let alone your
precious aesthetics.

Play along & you, too
will have a place to create content in
(I)topia.

Self-identify
    & the <wink><wink>
        <nudge><nudge> algorithm takes off points for

INACCESSIBILITY
           then offers a free kick

      in the A [still in

          prototype]. Repeat one of the menu items
to make your claim
        or wait for one of our representatives to
state your claim for you.

     With an

    intergenerational
    bandit behind every

    butte   & a herd

     of sacred ribeyes

            on the horizon

there's no way to keep any brainchild
           on the rails.

     Whoa…our narrative's getting

CO-OPTED
      down at the co-op, we can
        feel it in our water, Scofflaw.

Times are tough. That ripple's

the end of a bubble, a period of "flux"
                    a moratorium on selling eloquent
mares to one another. Nothing but nags

                    & a circle of wagons

                    waving our flag, only not in the name
of

        timely aid, no.

                    We ain't been this spooked
            since the cavalry was coming.

                        Reverb the same refrain.

                                    Consider

your self under

                    new management though you will be
invited to stay on in a politically
gelded capacity. Never mind

                        (I) in the guise of a buzzing
hivemind still undecided on the fate of dandelions.

                    Scofflaw, settle your hash
                        & kiss these grits because help

                        is en route though you gotta steer clear of

eye contact with

                    Ally just let him do
                                all the talking.

Scofflaw groans, seeing the anvil
                          & mammatus clouds
           coming down.
He's too long in the tooth
               for the latest tornado
to photo-bomb his big day. Meanwhile, the hoofbeats
   of (I), Ally, & Big Other
   are beyond audible

Risparmiate lo scherno...
Della morte non mi metto pensiero
e ben voi tutti lo sapete!
Pistola o laccio è uguale...
Se mi sciogliete un braccio mi sgozzo di mia mano!
D'altro voglio parlarvi:
della donna che amo...

but the debt clock's well past high noon for our
lanky
      trickster
plum out of pancho tricks

                     & spaghetti themes

   bordering on uncool.

Scofflaw's quick but Ally's quicker in his Taiwanese moccasins

to leap into this played scenario

                                  & slow-clap

our singin' slinger

                    into complete hiatus.

HATE WASTE

A spot of housekeeping
as to what's to go out:

Here, we'd like to recognize
the extent of this
imaginary territory

recognize this specious
species of cryptolect
in this degradable
ragbag

commas with scorched
camouflage, tattered
tortoiseshells named
after the pattern
on the back of an
endangered turtle

pictures not of our kissers

chrysalises blown
after eclosion
escapees flown
into aspen cavities

Here, we'd like to recognize
what the Navajo say

about the black

       swallowtail

watching over

      the spirit.

Recognize that

      retract or redact

           is the interrogative.

    Back away slowly

        "first thought, best thought"

    even this font is

    ontological varmint

    roughly the pigment

    of Nabokov's know-how about blues

         he had never seen take flight.

Shred (do not shed

      one tear over)

   prickly rebuffs

   in a breast pocket

   with all the charm

   of a wartorn

      communiqué.

Here, we'd like to recognize

　　the young in one another's dysphoria

　　　wings that whirrrrr
　　　with the rustle
　　　of period
　　　　　　dresses
　　　with the bustle
　　　of sexed-up
　　　tremulation

　　　our checkered past
　　　our checkered whites

　　　outlets for our
　　　"earthing," plugging
　　　in our bedsheets

　　　letters of
　　　overweening
　　　affection tossed
　　　　　　as confetti
　　　stenciled grains
　　　of rice
　　　　　released
　　　from onion
　　　　　　glove.

Other images flap by. Crows
head from staging area
                    to concealed roost
    traverse a red sky…

Here, we'd like to recognize

usurer hangs cozener
what my cousin says
big crook put
little crook in
solitary

go against the grain
they run you down
go near an enclosure
they gun you down

Amherst in earnest
handing out plague
to the *wrong*
                Indians, exemplar
                        of *gnaritas nullius*
that unoccupied grey matter

that conspicuous imprint
windrow to soul erosion.

Here, we'd like to call it in

careless talk of
scalping law
stuck in our craw

consensual tactility
at anti-oppression
boot camp

that eldest organism
the first to orgasm
persuasion
     & excrete
contagion
     out of the same
multitasker
     the ooze of every
       oleaginous phrase
proven to choke
& croak ozone

cochlear hairs
tickled to the limit of
sonic stimulation

this stupid pelvic response.

Here, a pelican
    lands upon the loch
        sifts through slime
           (for metaphors)
with gular pouch
slurping translation
    of planetary
        extirpation
           into goldmine:

    this sunken figurehead
    suspect chromaticism
    gloam upon zygoma
    of colloidal beauty
        mask

    this lust upon plasticrust
    this warm dispatch
      from slashes in
       ' distressed pants

      scraps of the unrequited
freighted back
        UNSALVAGEABLE
  selvage
      from the skein of thought
subject to grubby chop
      shop.

Here, we'd like to recognize

                              the freaking long poem
              we built over a heap
                          of bones
the same old story
of a Bring Your
Own Pillory
              approach

                          the mouth on us
                          full of uncouth
                                      anacoluthon
                          from an ancient tongue
                          for "does not follow"

the weather, with its
pathetic fallacy
uneasy as a
stomach full
of fritillaries
feeding on
              loosestrife
beneath a crowd
of mammatus clouds

the same old handbill nailed to telephone pole.

/ 44

CALLING ALL SCOFFLAWS

You could not miss an allochthon
in a shady corner of the territory
with enough swag in that flim-flam
swagger to getcher goat up. Nothing
could be more contrary to the truth.

No other feller has more oil for your
toil, more allusions for your confusion
more balm for your quivering limbs
more blessèd calm for your jim-jams.

Fed up with foreign parts
breaking down in your poems
flat out tired of seeing that
sty in your mind's eye
then jog on down to the
nearest re-education
station for a free metacog
(worth 350 social credits).

If you are not 100% satisfied
in 15 days, notify one of our
agents. Confidentiality will be
monitored for quality assurance.

GLOBAL TRANSPLANT

Scofflaw's renewed for another season.
                              Bless the leverets for
teaching him how to
                    leap   from portal

                                        to portal
you can't keep a good ham down. Like any magpie
                    on the rump of a buffalo, he hopes for
symbiosis, relations more causal
              than casual.   Ethnography tells us
                    the weight of a heart   feels too
                    cheap an entry fee (stuck

                                        under

                        tongue)

no anechoic chamber
                    to plash cedar tea against—

    whoa...tread softly you tread upon my nightmares.

                        This is the voice of Bogus-Logos
cheerleading fertilization of a mind
                            raked into mob mentality against
personal style. To tentacle never even comes close to recombinant love
our jam let's call a clade a clade in this phyla of half-mad admirers over
the moon for this brand of oracular

smack

   down stitched together at the eleventh
hour for female trees in flower
 for field of flax
            set aflame by rhetorical flourishes

        more sonic than semantic

        anti-ghazal latitude shears
        hearsay denunciation
        codified gratification
        with black ·
         list ant
                acid relief for trickle down
     whisper
            torture
                S'all good till it's you

this crackdown on compositional intricacies
    Janáček's "Intimate Letters" (mildly) unrequited

      alto sul ponticello

                  but the older guy hooting approval
has so much
            Cansplainin' to do. First, the traditionalist must weigh
heart on ocean floor
            before innermost can be

yanked out—   "Better out than in"

           moans our slogan, not to spoil the mood

or spit in the

           kefir, not to downplay the pressing need for
           take-believe, a whole whack of transformations
           line our pockets from across imaginary 49th
                   stony faced

           paddlers fastforwarding pre-colonial ticktock
           with prophecies to jumpstart animal heart
           too jarring for stowaways or stragglers.

Look, just what is your dog in this hunt, Scofflaw?

PUNCTURE

A   hole

                in blackened chrysalis
meets the field of our view
about the proportions
of a legal loophole

            YEA BIG

property through which drained

wetland was dragged.

    We agree to

           KEEP   OUT

creeping by space-age flanks of monster
home compound
           {under
                  construction...}
                      we peep
through that hole, cite the predictive factors
for social parasitism, plain & simple. Scofflaw
      says caterpillars of certain blues
      mingle among red ant larvae
      mimic the queen if necessary.

Not for the first time, he loses the plot
leaves twelve hundred labours
leaves counting
the number of
                white
                        moths a chipping sparrow

can knock back

(hundreds?) falling short of
hyperbole attributable to the latest Muse in wide
                        cycling pants trammelling character arc
        under that tread worse for wear in need of repair
before she can be tossed up into minor

                constellation.

                        Never mind, with allies like these...

Jesus, another exegesis—you always gotta

                                pour milk on the
                        dictionary for breakfast, Scofflaw?
Picture the sole survivor of our

spectacular catastrophe

                being a tardigrade. No more
simian faces scratched upon cave surface. No more
mammalian
        lily dipping currents of a

                        boggletastic

        universe.

Another pat on the back for our capacity

                  for self-annihilation. Back in the day,
nothing was safe as houses, this nuclear family with digital
        Xanadu, hunkering
                  down in bunker

basking in splendid

              blue light. If that ain't progress, then I sho

don't know what is.

       True story. "Eyes" upon aftwing, a little wood nymph
flits by
        the comma perched upon poplar body
           with red-orange-yellow

        coquetry. Grail is the question

           mark stuck to slender basswood, or hanging
      from heart-shaped
         leaves, if not drunk on hops, or proboscis-deep
      in dung-
    heap.

More than once we wonder why you linger here, Scofflaw
why you set us dreaming of purple butterflies
                  just out of

                          reach?

A stern wind whistles

                    through his frame. His voice
barely audible, he recapitulates faint emanations of former as-
pirations

      the latest to see the Diversity

      Gardens before he goes

                UNDERGROUND.

Today the webinar's on how
certain kinds of punctuation

can puncture yer hopes.

            Notice there's no
                  etcetera butterfly.

As for the colourful question marks, we take 'em for notches
on a perfectly viable career path.

BOT RUSSE

Up & atomize

Repeat after We

"And one beauty cancels another"

[Start] mugging for the struggle sesh

Double down on double plus good

Mask & lock down your love

Mind what you Like

Prune your public tsundoku with care

Shame-tag your Friends with discretion

Elbow-pump your followers with gusto

Keep eye contact with body language experts

Never let them hear you flush

Learn to identify every species of "Karen"

Incentivize suffering with subdivided bribes

Run it up the flagpole & see who sets it alight

"Defund the thought police"

Disown the previous statement

Disavow the heavy-breathing heart-clickers

Namaste the crap out of the others

Minimize the frame for best results

Influence better than their influence

Elect I, Bot Russe, for Badass

Burn notice all guilt-ridden assets

Fondle the business end of Fragility

Watch the chewy nougat essence flow outward

Exhale the same refined sugar charlatanism

Trade in "Choose Your Own Adventure" trademark

Quash all sales of *Jen Mod Hears a Genocide*

Dismantle all canon fodder

"And one beauty cancels another"

Tell me what my Maundy Monday's like

Abort all ruling class sports

Torch the Angel of History

Slay the names slay the names

Spray the face of Cervantes

Remove all Debussy from your hybrid

Report to your new local Chieftain

Accept no substitute jersey slogans

Avoid all sensitive key areas

Combinations of 2-0-4-6

"One country, two systems"

"Rockin' in the Free World"

Taiwan on a bomber jacket

Hong Kong in your kitchen dance upload

Render any fact as a live-streaming easter egg

Multitask as little red masculinity campaign

Replace with the closest climate coach

Remember not to stray too far from the script

"Kick the racism out of racists"

Flambé that vocal fry in the pan

Filet the violence out of silence

Rebrand as Org for Love & Empathy (OLE)

Terminate the mutes

Flay the daylights out of stragglers

Race to the bottom in record time

Recant mercantilism on the way home

Cap social capitalism in the A

Keep the eco-friendly T-shirt

Robo-voice dissent as classic dissonance

"And one beauty cancels another"

Do not repeat your mantra out loud

(Blacklists matter)

List under Top Ten Horror Comedies

Set comfort level on [Squirm]

Munch on the monarchy from within

Reprogram unclear football codes

Repurpose nuclear family model

Add "Freedom Kneebenders" to cart

Check skull sizing chart for impactful outcomes

Accept surcharge for Uighur ~~slave~~ labour

Use two bits on a string to increase credits

Inform on neighbourhood gatherings

Win countless prizes in social currency

Firebomb bricks & mortar for Nazi verification

Total all sh*t our interiority sez

Storyboard novel contagion arc

> *If we in our affect*
>
> *dance where no one peeps*
>
> *singing each to each:*
>
> *"I am emoji, emoji*
>
> *emoji born to be*
>
> *real feels bludgeon"*

Censor any anti-viral spirals gone viral

Wander lonely as a social bearing cloud

Reel in all bonspiel super-spreaders

Reboot apology tour with ethical breathables

Rebrand each synthetic as "bend sinister"

Report this poem to your nearest association

Shed toxicity for the snake plant

Shoo away the net-runoff cloud

Scoff the law & the law coughs

"And one beauty cancels another"

THE OTHER SIDE (I) SEEN

One day we get wind of the factoid the Air's changed
                         (say fake news one more time

            I can't even)

                    we feel it in Scofflaw's

        gangly

                    stride, comment on his being more laconic
            than the first Laconian only before you say Lacanian put it
            out of your noggin coz our cuz

                            was quick
                                    on the draw in a random way
'specially when on a randonnée

or swelling in the belly of the nearest coach house

poaching the finest axes to grind in these parts

pried loose from the leaky roof of the Nattersphere.

There's no way our man's running back to Scratchback

that's for durned sure, or so the talk goes.

Same day we get wind about Air, we hear Scofflaw's

decamped like a thief in the dark with Business

Inklish in tow.

            Funny Business, we call him.

Now for

        the record we never did trust Inklish, a shifty
fidgety type who boosted lame thoroughbreds
before making the move to pinching lame papers
on finer subtleties of the language

NO IDEAS

but his own

We'd seen him stagger around town
with Staggolee, this administrator

              of Authenticity
unless we're putting fart before horse—ha!

    Fixing to go, Scofflaw squeezes our cheeks
kisses our temples
          & blubbers
      over
         our rubbernecking before he flags down

the bus with

      a tongue-flogging to keep a joggerly pace
so he can spew
    his latest views on *Der
    unterbrochene Gedanke*
& we're like, Scofflaw
       this ain't no time for pesky
               Penderecki.

His testy riposte:

       It's always time for pesky Penderecki.

       That quartet for clarinet

           & strings never yet failed
to put me in an ambiguous
                mood.
   We run
        alongside until the stitches in our sides
get the better of us.
               Say the names
               say the names, Scofflaw roars
over the exhaust, with a caveat:
            If you have a name
              you can be sold
              you can be told
           by that name leave, or come
             you become, in short
           a reference, or if bad luck
            is large in your future
         you might become an institution.

We'd prefer to defer to
one of the Mauss-Strauss bunch

them reputable studiers
of the half-savage mind

for behind their citations

twitches this twisted

> homunculus
> hanger-on.

For origin story, try a chilling threnody
in the rare, unexpurgated edition

out back of Hassbein, Saskatchewan

where the mustard's been having it off

with the canola for as long as the eye

> can roll...

Business Inklish owns this notion

straight out of the gate like a boss
mindful of mobbing should the Air
> whiff that way
bordering on
> *social perturbation.*

Thing is, Scofflaw with his Divining
> Water™   & thinky inklings

ought to have gotten one of his hunches

there was nothing kosher about

this little imp from the time he was no bigger
than an avant-garde squiggle
wiggling among the weeds

snuggling up to
misadventures & sundry
Scofflaw (purportedly) had had.

Business Inklish, with a voice that drips syrupy turpitude
pleads his attributes:
Speaking cacographically

Eye bean 2 sCrawl Kollej
test my mettle go on, invigilate the

proceedings, Scofflaw
you'll find me an open book
that goes by
Benedict S. Inklish (to quench your
curiosity, the big "S" stands
for "Succotash").

Scofflaw, I don't expect you've taken
one

gander at my blog, but I can give you the skinny. Just look
how we've been in lockstep

since the hour of our respective birthings

under the same lorn star, each emerging with an imprint
with the same outfit in the same year, then being up
for the same laurels
though your star has a mite
more polish to its spectral wavelength than the shine o' mine
or so I reckon.

Their shadows growing longer, when are they going
to kick aside that tin of overheated

BEINGS

& double up in the same Mountain
Hardwear Hotbed
                    to conserve
sang
    froid?

            Keep in mind, whenever two vowelpokes
                hit the happy trails, their business is their business
                    but in such a tinderbox climate, we are obliged

                to provide a disclaimer for every ferro rod.

Business Inklish is a day shy of ageless
& in a year or two hopes are high he'll

blossom into an adult in touch with
his own high-mindedness

                            a crack parser at ten
                            paces with adroitness

        with any heap
        of metadata

                        able to divide academician
    from macadamia milk
within minutes, though it may be sour crêpes
    we never had no higher learnin'.

The squees wearing off, Funny Business
gets down to brass tacks.

Tomorrow in the tussle
think on me, Scofflaw
you who sent me   a sans-serif form letter

declaring

     LOVE
       IS
     FORM
             you who clamped in mind

                    forged   fetters

             you who drowsed when

browsing my

          gallery of frowy-faces…

This apocryphal yarn shows him
full of beans
to cull   wheelbarrows of

                    utterances

from the lexicon upon pain of
dearth, taking aim at the Gun
Runner's Decal for ethical
discourse in a comfy chair.

Commentators within earshot designate the next
second as the sketchiest blur in the history of ligature aside from this
rapid-fire aside:

> *You're a one-eyed jack in these parts, but (I) seen the other side*
> *of your face.*

Some swear he cultivates his pri-
vate stash in an ankle holster to bolster his word-hoard

if not a lavish pen below the
gaze of his navel, the sort that knew the shape of how
Nations slip & slide, or how news blows into town
third-hand, or even in tenfold gusts of that
jocoserious   lexicon

standoff.

Business Inklish blasts so fast
before the conceptual blanks
get there, he's already
washing his hands of another

fait de complicité

with a generous spume of

CERTAINTY
FOAM

then a half-dozen squeezes of sanitizer on the other side
of the boujee boutique   double doors.

Hours or years later, the aftermath
of this proprioceptive sidestep is
this can(n)on backfiring in the
stumped face of BS Inklish
with braintwiddlers, stubblejumpers
                              & a bright burst of
verbiage outside his specialty.
                         Call it appropriation

       in reverse whittled

              down into verse
                              faster than your average
disaster Business Inklish
                      is losing syllabi

then l o o s e n i n g up

                      in the molecular

sense. A few pieces of silver survive the process
just to give the myth a certain something.

       Never let 'em see yer frets

          & never show yer hand, Scofflaw yawns

no matter how sanitized you count on

being

      WHAT YOU CAN'T SEE
              CAN HURT YOU

For the unstudied
                    frazzled by nifty sleight of hand
lateralized brainin' mainly rebounds any fricassee
come your way, swaps every plain word for
                              grade A udderance
dashing nomenclatures
with minimal clatter
                    to the ground. Appears to
layfolk like a whopping manifesto

                              made manifest

& echoes like fast-acting tactical karma

in a jam jar, no known side effects

aside from

        COMPLEAT

    defeat.

Soft now.   See the gaggle of pendraggers waddle
                    this way and that, leaving the spines of

    various succulents

                        upon compost heap

        in memory of

                    Funny Business, the most
    anarchic customer to ever hitch up
                              tenured britches.

The only way to keep it real:
rustle up a colonial cochineal
muss the lips of a lady with
said product

       to keep the legend of Scofflaw alive
on many a used serviette

before he trips
       off the grid
leaving us high & dry
in another
      HIATUS.

In other words, there's something in our eye
whenever the wind's still
           too still   without the susurrus
    of his epic
    gassing
       storming the fortified

borough of our

      hard-won affection.

Follow the
    WANTED
       circulars of Kounter
Kultural workers to fingernail

his whereabouts

through conundrums & doldrums alike.

Best bet, he's linked up

with semi-known scofflaws

at the border of untariffed speech

                           if not at the fringe
of formalized speakeasy, scuttling through
Underground Say-Load
                     with cartloads of rejections

(the only growth industry in them thar parts).

        Though even (I)'s gone strangely quiet.

Talk all you want to

               Time Mechanic

or Social Prescriber

 or a flutter of social butterflies

about the man with the plans

                 & you won't get nada

save his squirreling away rain cheques
towards an operatic taco franchise.

This, like most everything, is mere hearsay.

ACKNOWLEDGMENTS

Many thanks to the friendly folks at Anvil Press for publishing this storied text. Also thanks to KC Adams for lending us her birch-bark artwork for the cover backdrop.

Thanks to Sharon Thesen for switching me onto Edward Dorn, whose Gunslinger was a considerable spur to my posterior when beginning this book. Cheers to Kevin Connolly for his editorial advice on the Mach 1 archival version.

Special thanks to Michael Barnholden, whose sharpshooter eye and quick hands really made the text get up and dance.

A tip of the fedora to *Audeamus*, *Dispatches from the Poetry Wars*, *Partial Zine*, *Prairie Fire*, and "The Hauck" for publishing excerpts from the urtext of this book.

Elbow pumps to the Scofflaws in Treaty 13, who had my back at every twist and turn of the language.

ABOUT THE AUTHOR

Garry Thomas Morse is a two-time nominee for the Governor General's Award for his poetry collections, *Discovery Passages* and *Prairie Harbour*, and a two-time nominee for the ReLit Award for his speculative fiction novels, *Minor Episodes/Major Ruckus* and *Rogue Cells/Carbon Harbour*. His most recent titles are *Yams Do Not Exist* and *Scofflaw*. Morse has served as the 2018 Jack McClelland Writer-in-Residence at the University of Toronto, and as the 2019 Carol Shields Writer-in-Residence at the University of Winnipeg.